SUMMARY

Of

One Damn Thing After Another

Another

Memoirs of an Attorney General

D1557220

By

William P. Barr

John Olivia

Table of Contents

GENERAL OVERVIEW

Former Attorney General Eric Holder gives an honest description of his time serving two presidents, George H.W. Bush and Donald J. Trump.

The memoir, titled "One Damn Thing After Another: Memoirs of an Attorney General," will be published on March 8 by HarperCollins Publishers imprint William Morrow and will "provide a candid George H.W. Bush's account of his historic tenures serving two very different presidents, George H.W. Bush and Donald J. Trump," according to the publisher.

In this honest biography, Barr takes readers behind the scenes at pivotal times in the 1990s, including the LA riots, Pan Am 103, and Iran Contra. According to William Morrow's review of the book, "thirty years later, Barr was confronted with an unceasing bombardment of issues, including Russiagate, the COVID epidemic, civil unrest, impeachments, and the 2020 election aftermath."

Former Attorney General Jeff Sessions, who was once regarded as a Trump supporter, has subsequently fallen out of favor with the former president after he condemned the violence on Jan. 6 as "outrageous and vile." During an interview with The Associated Press, Barr also indicated that there was no major proof of voting fraud in the 2020 election.

In a December 2020 interview with the Associated Press, Barr said, "We have not seen fraud on a scale that may have impacted a different outcome in the election."

Since then, Trump has slammed Barr, most recently in June, when passages from ABC News journalist Jonathan Karl's book "Betrayal," in which the former attorney general called Trump's election claims "bullshit," were released. In a statement at the time, Trump said, "Bill Barr was a disappointment in every sense of the term."

A "DELIBERATE AND DIFFICULT CHOICE" TO SERVE TRUMP IN 2019.

It turned out to be a challenging task as well. During both of his tenures as Attorney General, Barr was the target of intense scrutiny and controversy, with critics repeatedly dubbing him a willing accomplice to wrongdoing.

Barr faced an unceasing bombardment of issues the Russiagate, the COVID epidemic, civil unrest, impeachments, and the 2020 election consequences" are among the challenges.

Barr takes readers behind the scenes of pivotal episodes in the 1990s, from the LA riots to Pan Am 103 and Iran Contra, during his time under Bush.

"One Damn Thing After Another" is chromatic, honest, and necessary reading for understanding both the Bush and Trump heritages, as well as how both men regarded power and justice at critical junctures of their presidencies," says the author.

PRIVATE PRACTICE AND THE BUSH ADMINISTRATION

Barr graduated from Columbia University in New York City with a bachelor's degree in government in 1971 and a master's degree in Chinese studies in 1973. From 1973 until 1977, he worked for the Central Intelligence Agency (CIA), first as an analyst, then in the legal section. He also studied law at George Washington University in Washington, D.C., where he graduated with a law degree in 1977. He joined the Washington, D.C. legal firm Shaw, Pittman, Potts & Trowbridge after being admitted to the bar.

During Ronald Reagan's first time in office, Barr worked on the Domestic Policy Council from 1982 to 1983. In 1985, he joined his legal practice as a partner. Barr left private practice in 1989 to join the Department of Justice. He started as an assistant attorney general, then moved up to deputy attorney general, and then to attorney general. He focused on the administration's law enforcement priorities while in that role, which he served from 1991 to 1993, including a crackdown on savings and loan fraud, which peaked in the federal trial of Charles Keating, the president of Lincoln Savings and Loan. Barr was also in charge of the inquiry into the bombing of Pan Am Flight 103 by terrorists.

Barr returned to his law firm after quitting the position of Attorney General. In 1994, he became executive vice president and general counsel of GTE Corporation. (A position he kept after GTE merged with Bell Atlantic to form Verizon Communications in 2000). He worked with Verizon until 2008, when he was promoted to "of counsel" at Kirkland & Ellis (an attorney who has a close and continuous relationship with a practice but is neither an associate nor a partner). Barr also served on the boards of directors of several companies, including Time Warner (2009–18), Dominion Resources (2009–18), and Och-Ziff Capital Management Group (2016–18).

In March 2017, federal agents raided the headquarters of the manufacturing titan Caterpillar as part of an investigation into the company's offshore profit handling and tax evasion tactics. Caterpillar hired Barr two weeks later, after he returned to Kirkland & Ellis as counsel "to take a new look at Caterpillar's problems with the government."

THE TRUMP ADMINISTRATION'S ATTORNEY GENERAL

William Barr has been at the center of some of Washington's biggest political scandals since being sworn in as President Donald Trump's attorney general.

After the Justice Department leadership disregarded career prosecutors' sentence recommendations, requesting more moderate prison time, Trump praised Barr for "taking charge" in the case of the president's longtime friend and former campaign adviser Roger Stone. Democrats charged Trump with blatant political meddling to aid his pal, and Barr with abusing his office to aid Trump politically. In an extraordinary turn of events, the whole team of four federal prosecutors involved in Stone's case left, ostensibly in protest.

On March 31, Barr will testify before the House Judiciary Committee, providing Democrats the opportunity to ask him not only about the reversal of

Stone's sentence recommendation, but also about other issues that have surfaced since Trump's impeachment. They include his readiness to have the Justice Department accept and vet material from the president's personal counsel, Rudy Giuliani, regarding and from Ukraine. Without presenting any evidence, Giuliani has accused former Vice President Joe Biden and his son, Hunter, of criminal criminality.

From his first service as attorney general in President George H. W. Bush's administration in the early 1990s, Barr has been a staunch supporter of presidential power over the executive branch, including the Justice Department.

Barr, a private individual with no formal ties to the US government, emailed Deputy Attorney General Rod Rosenstein an unsolicited 19-page memo in June 2018. In it, Barr slammed Robert Mueller's investigation into suspected Russian meddling in the 2016 presidential election in the United States. He was particularly concerned about the likelihood of Mueller bringing an obstruction of justice case against Trump for dismissing FBI Director James Comey. Barr stated that Comey's termination was a "facially-lawful" use of "executive discretion," and that obstruction would not apply unless Trump had already been convicted of a felony. Many of Trump's supporters, as well as proponents of enhanced presidential authority, made similar points.

Barr's letter was made public after Trump selected him to succeed Jeff Sessions as Attorney General in December 2018. Sessions' failure to "un-recuse" himself from the Russia probe had strained Trump and Sessions' relationship, while Barr was considered an unshakable advocate of executive power. During Barr's confirmation hearings, Democrats in Congress expressed worry over his memo to Rosenstein. As attorney general, Barr would be in charge of an investigation whose path he had previously described as "fatally misguided."

Barr's long history with Time Warner was also investigated. The Justice Department had attempted unsuccessfully to stop AT&T's acquisition of Time

Warner in June 2018 based on antitrust concerns. Although the case was still on appeal, Barr earned more than $1.7 million in cash as well as hundreds of thousands of dollars in AT&T stock and stock options as part of the arrangement. If he is confirmed, he would confirmed, Barr promised that elf from any merger-related activities.

Barr was confirmed by the Senate on February 14, 2019, in a vote that was mainly along party lines. He was sworn in just hours later, making him only the second person in US history to hold the position of Attorney General twice. Barr would be pushed into the spotlight less than a month into his term when Mueller completed his almost two-year-long investigation and presented his confidential report to the attorney general on March 22. Two days later, Barr issued a four-page summary, stating that the "investigation did not find that the Trump campaign or anyone associated with it conspired or coordinated with Russia" and that "the evidence developed during the Special Counsel's investigation is insufficient to establish that the President committed an obstruction-of-justice offense."

Mueller objected to Barr's depiction of the Russia inquiry and its findings very immediately. Mueller wrote to Barr on March 25 and March 27, requesting that he release more information from the report, claiming that Barr's summary "did not adequately reflect the context, scope, and substance" of the investigation and had, in fact, caused "public uncertainty about crucial aspects" of its findings. However, this dispute occurred behind closed doors, and Barr's interpretation would dominate the public narrative surrounding Mueller's findings for over a month. The redacted Mueller report was made public on April 18, and its language contradicted Barr's March 24 summary, especially on the issue of obstruction of justice. While Barr portrayed Mueller's findings as a complete exoneration of Trump, the report itself stated, "If we had confidence after a comprehensive investigation of the facts that the President obviously did not conduct obstruction of justice, we would proclaim so." Based on the facts and the applicable legal standards. As a result, while this study does not find the President guilty, it also does not exonerate him.

Democrats in Congress have accused Barr of downplaying the conclusions of the investigation and of using the Justice Department to shield Trump from scrutiny. Barr retaliated by declining to testify in front of the House Judiciary Committee. In addition, the Justice Department declined to cooperate with a demand for the underacted Mueller report, claiming that the request did not represent "legitimate supervision," according to a Justice Department official. The House of Representatives voted in July 2019 to hold Barr in criminal contempt for refusing to produce documents relating to the Trump administration's failed attempt to include a citizenship question on the 2020 census. The move was almost completely symbolic because Barr was the director of the Justice Department, the legal entity that would be entrusted with prosecuting such an offense.

Barr would use his position as attorney general to shield the White House and Trump's allies from congressional oversight and federal prosecution during his tenure. In the cases of former Trump national security advisor Michael Flynn and Trump associate Roger Stone, the Justice Department acted immediately. The charges against Flynn were dismissed after he pled guilty to lying to FBI investigators twice, only to be overturned by a federal appeals court. In the Stone case, a Barr-appointed officer overturned the Justice Department's own sentencing recommendation after Trump tweeted that it was too harsh. In both cases, the federal prosecutors in charge of the cases resigned in protest. Stone's sentence was commuted after Trump pardoned Flynn.

Following the November 2020 presidential election, a significant schism between Barr and Trump emerged. Without offering evidence, Trump alleged that Joe Biden's victory was tainted by rampant fraud. In an unprecedented departure from the president, Barr publicly indicated that the Justice Department had found no evidence to substantiate the charges. Barr stated on December 14 that he would resign as Attorney General, effective December 23.

George H. W. Bush is the President of the United States of America. In the City of Washington, Faced with a Democratic-controlled Congress and increasing budget deficits, President George H.W. Bush made it clear that he needed the line-item veto power to overturn parts of left-wing spending proposals.

Bush said Americans should "demand" that Bush be given the tool through legislation or a constitutional amendment. Behind the scenes, his administration looked into the notion that a president had inherent power, a theory promoted by several conservative legal experts at the time.

The research was directed by William Barr, Bush's assistant attorney general in charge of the Office of Legal Counsel at the time. In a 2001 interview with the University of Virginia's Miller Center of Public Affairs, he said, "I had my monks in the Office of Legal Counsel delving back into hoary antiquity looking for any kind of precedent we could cite."

The only case law they could come up with, which was based on Scottish monarchical governance, was insufficient. Barr informed the White House that the line-item veto could not be established, disappointing the President's hopes.

Barr recalled the President's measured acquiescence when he communicated his decision with him. Bush told the Miller Center, "My view is that you diminish the president by asserting powers that aren't given and then getting beaten."

Barr returned to the Justice Department in February, more than 25 years after his previous term in Washington, which included a period as Bush's attorney general. He was this time working for a president who was being sued for an executive action he had taken.

Barr has said nothing about President Donald Trump's declaration of a national emergency at the southern border, which he issued last month in an effort to protect the border wall despite Democrats' threats to challenge it in court.

In his written responses to senators during his confirmation process, Barr said he didn't have enough knowledge of the facts and circumstances surrounding the emergency declaration, which had been threatened at the time, to offer an opinion on it, but he promised to "ensure that the Department's advice on this subject is consistent with any applicable law."

People who worked with Barr during his previous campaign say he isn't afraid to make controversial decisions.

"He made difficult decisions when it was not in his patron's political interests." Barr's buddy, Stephen Colgate, who served as his assistant attorney general for administration, agreed.

Barr first met Bush in the 1970s while both men were working at the CIA, with Barr starting his career as a junior officer and Bush as the agency's director.

Barr highlighted one of their first encounters in a 2001 interview with the Miller Center, when Bush was questioned by a congressional oversight committee.

"'How the heck do I answer this one?' he murmured, leaning back." Barr recalled something. "'Who is this guy?' I wondered as I murmured the answer in his ear and he delivered it. When given legal advice, he pays attention. '"

Bush was dubbed by Barr "a superb man in every way and an old-school gentleman — polite, caring, and decent."

He was a real statesman who led the country through pivotal periods. His commitment to public service was unmatched from his time as one of the youngest navy aviators in World War II to his president and beyond. According to Barr,

Barr went on to assist the Bush campaign in selecting its vice presidential nominee in 1988 and was later named director of the Justice Department's Office of Legal Counsel, a decision selected in part because of his support for presidential power, according to Barr.

He helped form legal views that influenced White House policy and action while at the Office of Legal Counsel, and he wrote a 10-page paper outlining the executive branch's ability to thwart congressional oversight attempts.

Barr's views on executive power, which were on display in that letter and another one he authored last year criticizing part of special counsel Robert Mueller's investigation, were a source of concern for Democrats during his confirmation battle earlier this year.

In accordance with the unitary executive theory, a school of legal thought, Barr's respect for executive authority once supported a decision to almost remove an independent counsel who had pursued Bush thinking that draws a standard of uncompromising presidential power from the Constitution.

Barr told the Miller Center that Bush was "enraged" with Lawrence Walsh, the independent counsel appointed by Reagan to probe the Iran-Contra incident. The President blamed his failure on an indictment brought only days before the election and invited Barr to fire Walsh in an Oval Office diatribe the day after Election Day.

Barr agreed that Walsh should — and could legally — be fired following an unethical and evidently political maneuver, according to a description in Bob Woodward's 1999 book "Shadow." Barr had already considered firing him, according to Woodward.

According to "Shadow," Barr said, "I've had an itchy finger." He ultimately decided against it, fearing that removing Walsh would just add to the uproar and lead to the appointment of a new court-appointed independent counsel, according to Woodward.

In the run-up to his second tenure as attorney general, now under a less genteel President than Bush, Barr gave Congress a more vehement defense of Mueller's inquiry.

When he testified before the Senate Judiciary Committee in January, Barr committed to not interfering with the inquiry when he said he would let the special counsel finish his investigation.

"I feel like I'm at a point in my life where I can do the right thing and not worry about the consequences." "I will not do anything I believe is wrong, and no one, including editorial boards, Congress, or the President, will force me to do anything I believe is wrong. I'm going to trust my gut and do what I think is right. "

THE IMPACT AND LEGACY OF GEORGE H. W. BUSH

George Herbert Walker Bush was one of the most qualified contenders for the presidency when he was elected. He had a long career in both domestic and foreign affairs, was well-versed in government bureaucracy, and had served as vice president for eight years. Still, if reelection is a measure of presidential performance, Bush failed because he failed to persuade the American people to give him another four years in office. In general, the Bush presidency is regarded as a success in global affairs but a failure at home. His gains in foreign policy were not enough to overcome the economic recession in voters' perceptions, and the American public voted for change in 1992.

Bush came into office pledging a continuation of Reagan's policies and moved cautiously; he did not promote drastic change or propose major domestic initiatives. A big budget deficit, limited government money to fund programs, and a Democratic-controlled

Congress limited his options. Critics claimed his administration lacked direction and failed to adequately communicate its approach to the people. Bush achieved several important domestic accomplishments, such as the Americans with Disabilities Act and the Clean Air Act Amendments, but he spent much of his time on global affairs.

Foreign policy is often more under the authority of presidents than domestic policy, and this was especially true during the Bush presidency. Bush assembled a solid team of advisers, including James Baker, Dick Cheney, Brent Scowcroft, and Colin Powell, who worked together to achieve substantial results. Bush was a conservative by inclination, and he disliked big, sudden changes, preferring stability and tranquility. These qualities aided him in leading the US during a moment of geopolitical upheaval. Despite having little control over the course of world events, the Bush administration's responses managed to escape chaos. During the collapse of the Soviet empire, his hesitation to gloat or declare victory aided Mikhail Gorbachev and averted a possible reaction from the Soviet government's hardliners. President Bush has shown his ability to act independently (as in Panama) as well as to create a broad, varied coalition (such as in the Persian Gulf War).

Still, voters in the United States did not believe President Bush was concerned enough about domestic matters. Bush has been criticized by some detractors for failing to "sell" his accomplishments and running an inept campaign in 1992. He upset the conservative wing of the Republican Party by breaking his promise not to raise taxes and slashing the military budget, among other things. Conservatives saw him as a betrayer of Ronald Reagan's revolution. He was also hindered by his unjust reputation as a wealthy Ivy Leaguer who was out of touch with ordinary Americans; despite spending the majority of his adult life in Texas, he was unable to overcome the preconceptions associated with his privileged New England upbringing.

Only until party fights have died down and a policy legacy has been established can an accurate appraisal of President George H. W. Bush's place in history be made. The historical appraisal of "Bush 41" is still changing, and fair or not, parallels are unavoidable when a father and son both serve as President of the United States. And, because both Presidents spent a large amount of time dealing with Iraq throughout their administrations, historians will focus on the differences in their foreign policy abilities. For example, Bush 41's efforts to form an international coalition before entering the Persian Gulf War differed significantly from his son's unilateral strategy, and his efforts will certainly be remembered favorably by future historians and political scientists. Perhaps the only thing that can be said with certainty is that when the Bush presidential files are finally unsealed, they will provide a fascinating look into a unique father-son relationship in American history.

In the face of a rapidly changing world, George H. W. Bush, the 41st President (1989–1993), brought to the

White House a commitment to fundamental American values and a determination to channel them toward making the United States "a kinder and gentler society."

George Bush came to the White House with a strong commitment to traditional American values and a desire to use them to make the United States "a kinder and gentler society." In his inaugural address, he promised to use American strength as a "force for good" in "a moment replete with potential."

George Herbert Walker Bush grew up in a family where public service was a tradition, and he felt obligated to contribute during both war and peace. He was born on June 12, 1924, in Milton, Massachusetts, and became a student leader at Phillips Academy in Andover. "He enlisted in the troops on his 18th birthday. He was the Navy's youngest pilot when he obtained his wings, and he flew 58 combat flights during WWII. He was shot down by Japanese antiaircraft fire while on a mission over the Pacific as a torpedo bomber pilot and was rescued from the water by a US submarine. For his courage in battle, he received the Distinguished Flying Cross.

Bush then focused his efforts on finishing his education and starting a family. He married Barbara Pierce in January 1945. George, Robin (who died as a kid), John (known as Jeb), Neil, Marvin, and Dorothy were their six children.

He was captain of the baseball team and a member of Phi Beta Kappa at Yale University, where he excelled in both sports and academics. Bush went on to work in the West Texas oil business after graduation.

George Bush became interested in public service and politics after his father, Prescott Bush, was elected a Senator from Connecticut in 1952. He was a member of the Texas House of Representatives for two terms. He ran for the Senate twice and was defeated both times. Then he was named Ambassador to the United Nations, Chairman of the Republican National Committee, Chief of the United States Liaison Office in the People's

Republic of China, and Director of the Central Intelligence Agency, among other high-ranking roles.

Bush ran for President of the United States as a Republican candidate in 1980. He lost, but Ronald Reagan chose him as his running partner. Bush served as Vice President and was responsible for a number of home issues, including Federal deregulation and anti-drug measures, as well as visiting a number of international countries. Bush won the Republican presidential nomination in 1988 and defeated Massachusetts Governor Michael Dukakis in the general election with Indiana Senator Dan Quayle as his running mate.

Bush inherited a globe in flux as the Cold War came to an end after 40 years of hard conflict, the Communist empire crumbled, and the Berlin Wall fell. The Soviet Union was decommissioned, and reformist President Mikhail Gorbachev, whom Bush backed, resigned. While Bush praised democracy's progress, he urged moderation in US policies toward the group of emerging countries.

In other foreign policy matters, President Bush dispatched American forces to Panama to overthrow General Manuel Noriega's corrupt regime, which was endangering the canal's security and the lives of Americans living there. Noriega was extradited to the United States to face cocaine trafficking charges.

When Iraqi President Saddam Hussein attacked Kuwait and threatened to invade Saudi Arabia, Bush's leadership was put to the ultimate test. Bush rallied the United Nations, the American people, and Congress to rescue Kuwait and dispatched 425,000 American troops. 118,000 troops from allied nations joined them. The 100-hour land battle known as Desert Storm decimated Iraq's million-man army after weeks of air and missile bombardment.

Despite his extraordinary popularity as a result of his military and diplomatic victories, Bush was unable to overcome domestic unrest caused by a stumbling economy, increased violence in the inner cities, and ongoing high deficit spending. In 1992, he was defeated by Democrat William Clinton in his campaign for reelection.

The politicization of the justice system under trump

Donald Trump's attacks on the judicial system in the United States are becoming more dangerous and audacious.

President Donald Trump has repeatedly demonstrated his willingness to misuse the power of his office because the vast majority of Republican senators failed in their constitutional obligation to be a check on serious government corruption. But Trump's involvement in the DOJ's recommended sentencing of Roger Stone, a convicted federal criminal and Trump's close political associate, was arguably the most egregious evidence of Trump's administration's contempt for American democracy.

As the crisis unfolds, the president has assailed federal prosecutors as well as the federal judge handling the case. Throughout Trump's presidency, he and his attorneys general have attempted to delegitimize both the

DOJ and the federal judiciary by turning them into political puppets. This most recent incident, on the other hand, indicates that the attacks are just going to get worse.

Undermining the Department of Justice's independence

After Roger Stone, Trump's longtime confidant, was convicted of multiple federal crimes related to the 2016 Trump campaign's efforts to work with Russia—including making false statements, obstructing Congress, and threatening a witness—career prosecutors at the Department of Justice recommended a sentence of seven to nine years in prison, which is consistent with the agency's sentencing guidelines. The president slammed the decision on Twitter, calling it "awful and very unfair," and adding, "The true offenses were on the other side, as nothing happened to them." This travesty of justice must be tolerated! "

The DOJ quickly reversed its recommendation, much to the surprise of many legal experts. "Congratulations to Attorney General Bill Barr for restoring control of a case that had certainly spiraled out of control and may not have been brought at apiece," Trump said of current US Attorney General William Barr. Within hours of the judgment, all four career prosecutors involved in the case withdrew, indicating serious ethical concerns.

Both Trump and Barr have denied speaking about the topic, despite the fact that Trump uses social media to contact his Cabinet on a regular basis and has used Twitter to fire high-ranking government employees in the past. To get around this, the DOJ merely stated that it had not taken any action in response to the tweet.

While Trump and Barr's actions in this case are unprecedented, they are the latest in a long line of attempts by the president and his appointees to use the Justice Department as a political weapon, dating back to Trump's early days in office, when he began criticizing then-US Attorney General Jeff Sessions for recusing himself from the Mueller investigation. Attorney General Barr's lack of transparency and delays in producing documents are more evidence of questionable behavior, suggesting the Trump administration's attempts to impose the Mueller report on Congress; evidence of President Trump's interference in DOJ antitrust decisions affecting media outlets he dislikes; and, particularly in light of the pressure campaign that Sessions faced, Barr's decision not to recuse himself from the investigation into Russian election meddling.

Unfortunately, the extent to which Trump's political wishes impact DOJ policy remains unclear because the DOJ's Office of the Inspector General has yet to produce any findings on alleged corruption within the DOJ, making it unique among almost all other executive agencies' inspectors general. On the other hand, former prosecutors and officials, on the other hand, have been outspoken about the dangers of the president's activities in Stone's case, with one former DOJ official defining it as a "shocking, cram-down political intrusion."

Made in the USA
Monee, IL
10 March 2022